North Riverside Public Library District
2400 S. Des Plaines Avenue
North Riverside, IL 60546
708-447-0869
www.northriversidelibrary.org

DEADLY
MORGUES

by Joyce Markovics

Consultant: Ursula Bielski
Author and Paranormal Researcher
Founder of Chicago Hauntings, Inc.

BEARPORT
PUBLISHING

New York, New York

Credits

Cover, Kim Jones; TOC, © Darrin Kilmek/iStock; 4–5, © bytekontrol/iStock and © Kim Jones; 6, © Google 2017; 7, © Geoff Goldswain/Shutterstock; 8–9, © Roman Nerud/Shutterstock; 9B, © Gang Liu/Shutterstock and © Bertold Werkmann/Shutterstock; 10, © Photo Researchers, Inc/Alamy Stock Photo; 11, © Bridgeman Images; 10–11, © Josse Christophel/Alamy Stock Photo; 12, © Wellcome Images/CC BY 4.0; 13, © Private Collection/Archives Charmet/Bridgeman Images; 14, Public Domain; 15, © Mark Wells; 17, © Patrick Foto/Shutterstock; 18, © Christopher Payne/ESTO; 19, © Josh Partee.CC BY-SA 4.0; 20, © Kobbi R. Blair/Statesman-Journal/Associated Press; 21, © Thomas Patterson/The New York Times/Redux; 23, © zummolo/Shutterstock.

Publisher: Kenn Goin
Senior Editor: Joyce Tavolacci
Creative Director: Spencer Brinker
Photo Researcher: Thomas Persano

Library of Congress Cataloging-in-Publication Data in process at time of publication (2018)
Library of Congress Control Number: 2017007497
ISBN-13: 978-1-68402-270-0 (library binding)

For more information, write to Bearport Publishing Company, Inc., 45 West 21st Street, Suite 3B, New York, New York 10010. Printed in the United States of America.

10 9 8 7 6 5 4 3 2 1

CONTENTS

DEADLY MORGUES

You enter a cold room covered with dirty tiles. The lights flicker. You notice a metal stretcher against the wall. On it lies a body draped in a white sheet. A thin stream of blood trickles from the stretcher onto the floor. Then, suddenly, the lights go out!

Get ready to read four spine-tingling tales about deserted deadly **morgues**. Turn the page . . . if you have the nerve!

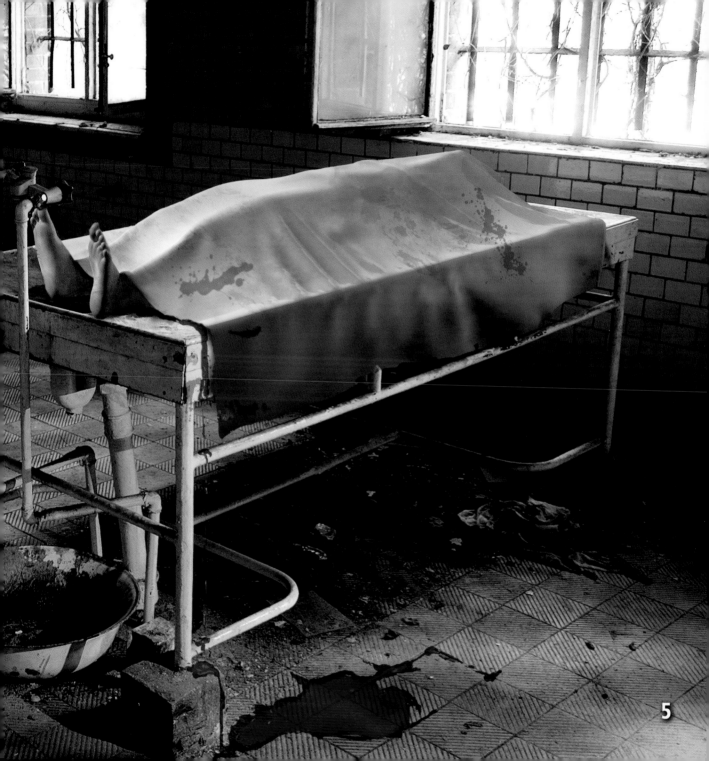

Stolen Body

Georgetown Morgue, Seattle, Washington

A morgue is often thought of as a creepy place. What if it's also the site of a terrible **crime**?

John "Figgy" Dorsey was a well-known jazz **musician**. He lived in Seattle with his wife. In 1947, John died suddenly. His body was then taken to the Georgetown Morgue. That's when the nightmare began.

Site of the Georgetown Morgue

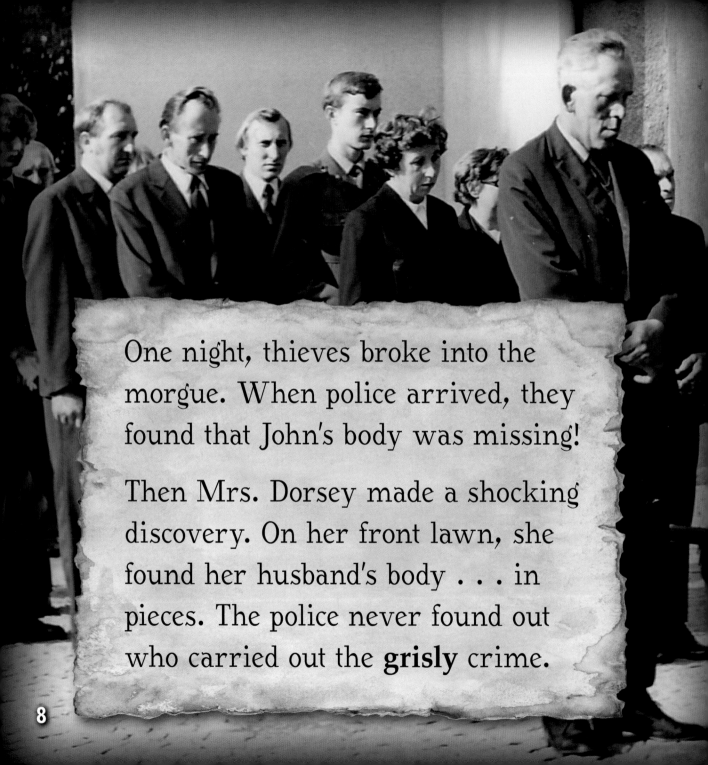

One night, thieves broke into the morgue. When police arrived, they found that John's body was missing!

Then Mrs. Dorsey made a shocking discovery. On her front lawn, she found her husband's body . . . in pieces. The police never found out who carried out the **grisly** crime.

Mrs. Dorsey sent the body parts back to the morgue. There, John's body was sewn back together—just in time for his **funeral**!

9

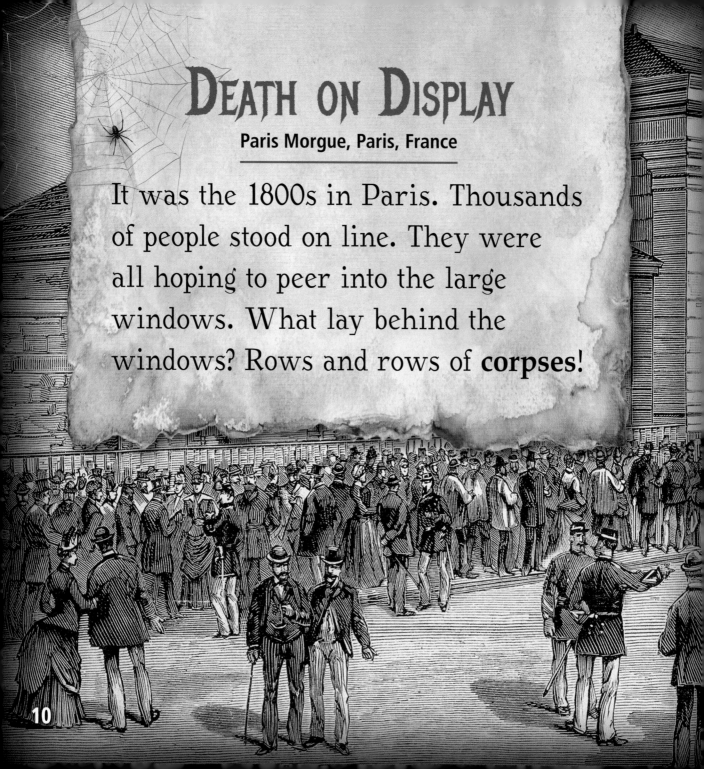

Death on Display

Paris Morgue, Paris, France

It was the 1800s in Paris. Thousands of people stood on line. They were all hoping to peer into the large windows. What lay behind the windows? Rows and rows of **corpses**!

The Paris Morgue

11

At the time, all the **unidentified** bodies in Paris were taken to the Paris Morgue. There, the corpses were put on stone blocks behind huge windows. Every day, people lined up to see the bodies. Some visitors came to find missing friends and family. Others came to simply **gawk** at the dead.

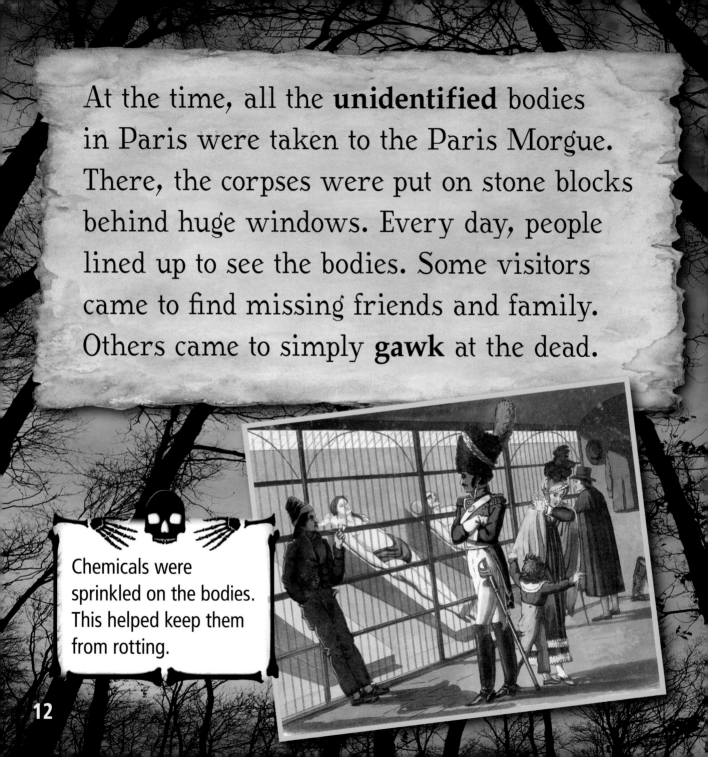

Chemicals were sprinkled on the bodies. This helped keep them from rotting.

13

MISSING!

Baxter Avenue Morgue, Louisville, Kentucky

Victor Vanderdark opened the Baxter Avenue Morgue in 1901. In 1932, he disappeared without a trace. Soon after, his only son, Warren, took over the morgue. Then Warren's wife **vanished**, along with their young daughter. Some people thought that Warren had killed his family.

Victor Vanderdark

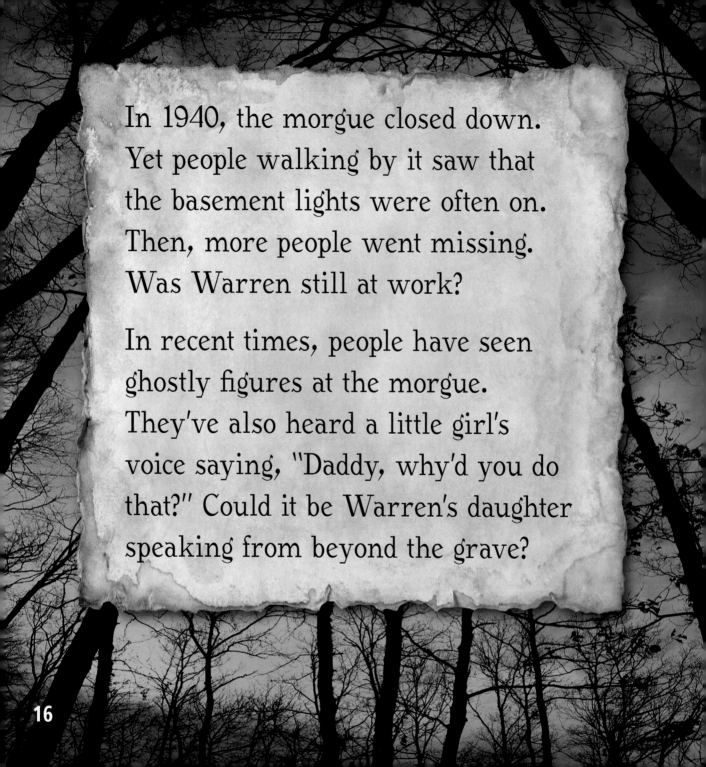

In 1940, the morgue closed down. Yet people walking by it saw that the basement lights were often on. Then, more people went missing. Was Warren still at work?

In recent times, people have seen ghostly figures at the morgue. They've also heard a little girl's voice saying, "Daddy, why'd you do that?" Could it be Warren's daughter speaking from beyond the grave?

In 1951, Warren Vanderdark also disappeared.

FORGOTTEN SOULS

Oregon State Hospital, Salem, Oregon

Stacked neatly in a dusty room at an Oregon hospital are thousands of small cans. Each one is carefully numbered. What's inside the cans? The answer will make your skin crawl.

The cans at the Oregon State Hospital

The Oregon State Hospital opened in 1883. Parts of it are still open today.

In the 1900s, thousands of sick people were sent to the hospital. Once there, they received poor care. Many died soon after arriving. Their bodies were **cremated** in the hospital morgue. Then the ashes were dumped into metal cans . . . and forgotten about.

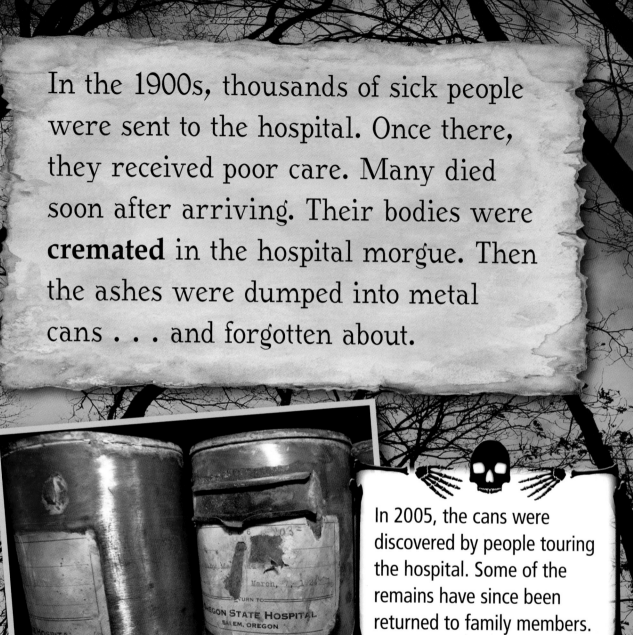

In 2005, the cans were discovered by people touring the hospital. Some of the remains have since been returned to family members.

21

Deadly Morgues
Around the World

GEORGETOWN MORGUE
Seattle, Washington

Check out a creepy morgue that's also a crime scene.

OREGON STATE HOSPITAL
Salem, Oregon

Learn about the terrible discovery of forgotten remains.

BAXTER AVENUE MORGUE
Louisville, Kentucky

Explore a mysterious and possibly haunted morgue.

PARIS MORGUE
Paris, France

Visit a place where the dead were on grisly display.

Arctic Ocean

NORTH AMERICA

EUROPE

ASIA

Atlantic Ocean

AFRICA

Pacific Ocean

Pacific Ocean

SOUTH AMERICA

Indian Ocean

AUSTRALIA

Atlantic Ocean

Southern Ocean

ANTARCTICA

GLOSSARY

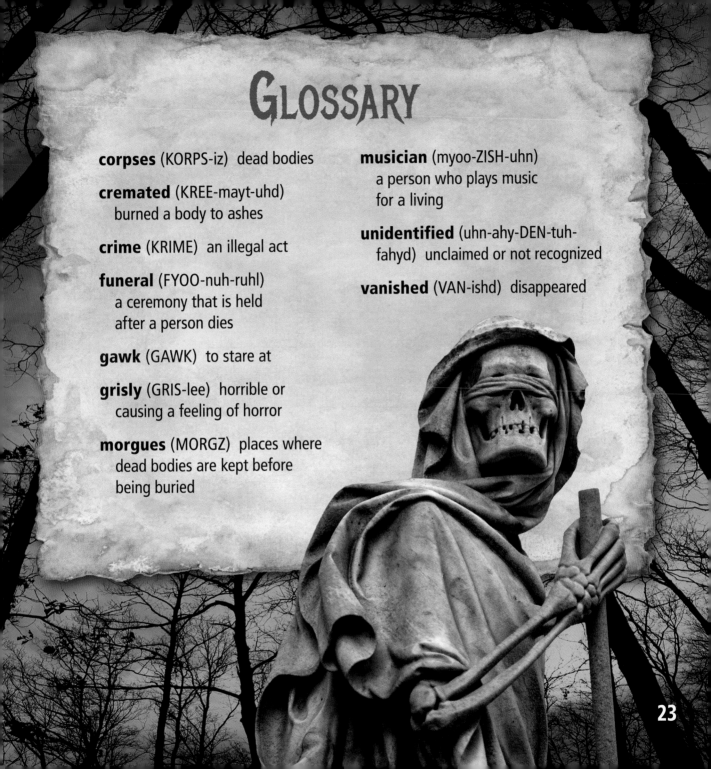

corpses (KORPS-iz) dead bodies

cremated (KREE-mayt-uhd)
  burned a body to ashes

crime (KRIME) an illegal act

funeral (FYOO-nuh-ruhl)
  a ceremony that is held
  after a person dies

gawk (GAWK) to stare at

grisly (GRIS-lee) horrible or
  causing a feeling of horror

morgues (MORGZ) places where
  dead bodies are kept before
  being buried

musician (myoo-ZISH-uhn)
  a person who plays music
  for a living

unidentified (uhn-ahy-DEN-tuh-
  fahyd) unclaimed or not recognized

vanished (VAN-ishd) disappeared

Index

Read More

Phillips, Dee. *Nightmare in the Hidden Morgue (Cold Whispers II).* New York: Bearport (2017).

Williams, Dinah. *Monstrous Morgues of the Past (Scary Places).* New York: Bearport (2011).

Learn More Online

To learn more about deadly morgues, visit:
www.bearportpublishing.com/Tiptoe

About the Author

Joyce Markovics lives in a 160-year-old house.
Chances are a few otherworldly beings live there, too.